YOUR INSTRUCTIONS...

This is a Dangermouse adventure with a difference! **YOUR** decisions decide whether or not Dangermouse succeeds in his latest assignment from Colonel K.

Start reading the book at page 1. At the end of every page you will find a number in brackets which tells you which page to turn to next. Sometimes you will have a choice to make. There will be a different number in the brackets against each choice. Having made your choice turn to the number of the page shown against it.

With your help (and Penfold's, of course!), Dangermouse must *completely* rid the world of some dangerous robots. If he fails, then you and Penfold can always try again!

GOOD LUCK!

St Michael

DANGER MOUSE

Illustrations by
Peter Campbell

story programme by
Allen Sharp

written by
Greg Steddy

Based on original material by
Brian Trueman

1

"What a wonderful day, eh, Penfold?" said Dangermouse cheerfully, bathing in the early morning sunshine that streamed through the window of his secret Mayfair residence.

He had just completed his usual three hundred press-ups, and the smell of toast was making him hungry.

"What's for breakfast?" he called. "I could eat a horse!"

"Sorry, DM," chuckled Penfold from the kitchen. "It won't fit in the toaster! You'll have to make do with toast and marmalade!"

"Righto," said Dangermouse. "I'm on my way."

But before he could move, a strange green cloud passed over the sun and blocked out the light.

"That's odd," muttered Dangermouse, with a puzzled frown. "There wasn't a cloud in the sky just now—and certainly not a green one!"

With a loud buzz, the videoscreen suddenly flashed on.
"Oh, no!" groaned Dangermouse. "That'll be Colonel K. Trust him to spoil my breakfast!"

"Morning, DM," said the Colonel briskly. "Not had your breakfast, you say? Too bad! Something urgent's cropped up and you'll have to deal with it right away!"
"What's the problem then, sir?" asked Dangermouse, trying to sound enthusiastic.
"Something very odd, DM," explained the Colonel. "All over the world, leading figures seem to be disappearing without trace! There have been reports of some sort of green ray that . . ."

His words were cut short as the videoscreen was filled with green light. Within seconds, Colonel K had vanished! (2)

2

At that moment, Penfold came rushing in with a look of panic on his face.

"You haven't burnt the toast *again*, have you?" sighed Dangermouse wearily.

"No, it's on the ceiling! Look!" cried Penfold. "Everything suddenly went green and up it went! It wasn't even ready!"

Dangermouse rushed to the window. The green cloud was passing directly overhead.

"I knew it!" he muttered grimly. "Ever heard of anti-gravity, Penfold?"

"No," replied Penfold blankly. "But I've got an Uncle Horace!"

Ignoring his hopeless assistant, Dangermouse revealed his theory: "Don't you see—first the world leaders, then Colonel K, and now the toast! I'm convinced that the cloud is the key to all this. It must be reversing the Earth's gravity and sucking everyone into it—rather like a giant magnet!"

"Crumbs!" cried Penfold, trying hard to knock the toast down with a broom handle. "I wish it would let go of my breakfast. I'm hungry!"

"No time to eat now," said Dangermouse firmly. "We've got to get after that cloud before it does any more harm. We'll take the space hopper!"

"But I can't go before breakfast," said Penfold miserably. "You *know* I always get hiccups if I try to do anything on an empty stomach!"

Should Penfold go with Dangermouse and do without his breakfast (7), or should he stay behind? (4) After all, the toast might hold as many clues as the green cloud!

3

"I wonder what Dangermouse is doing over there?" thought Penfold. "Still, I'd feel far safer with him than hanging round here on my own!"

He trotted towards the cave, but Dangermouse didn't seem to be at all pleased to see him.

"No time for questions now," he snapped. "Just hurry up, Penfold, before someone spots us!"

"Looks like I've put my foot in it again," thought Penfold. "I suppose he's cross with me for not staying where I was."

"Right, Penfold," said Dangermouse. "There's something very strange going on here, and I'm sure the answer lies in these caves. Now follow close behind me—it's very easy to get lost."

"But how do you know your way around, chief?" asked Penfold curiously.

Dangermouse didn't answer—he'd already raced down the nearest tunnel. Shrugging his shoulders, Penfold started after him. After all, he didn't want to be left on his own again.

Fortunately for Penfold, it wasn't dark. The walls of the tunnels seemed to glow with a greenish light, revealing a maze of tunnels and caves.

"I wish he'd slow down a bit," grumbled Penfold under his breath, as Dangermouse strode on ahead of him. "He *knows* I've only got short legs!"

He stopped briefly to catch his breath, but when he looked up, Dangermouse had disappeared!

"Oh crikey!" wailed Penfold. "He must have gone down that passage on the right. I'd better follow him before I get lost!" (10)

"All right, Penfold," said Dangermouse. "You can stay here if you want to, but I've got to find that cloud. I've a nasty feeling that Greenback may be up to his tricks again!"

"Gosh, thanks, chief!" cried Penfold, breathing a sigh of relief. "I'm sure I'd only get in the way!"

"Perhaps you're right," said Dangermouse. "It won't take me long to sort this out!"

Penfold watched as the space hopper soared away before going back to the kitchen to tackle his toast. Suddenly, the room filled with a strange green light.

"Oh crikey!" he wailed. "That rotten cloud's still after my breakfast! Why won't it leave me alone?"

The room began to spin, and to his horror Penfold felt himself begin to float upwards.

"Waagh! Help!" he squealed. "Put me down!"

He landed with such a bump that his glasses flew off. He groped around for them on the floor but, to his surprise, he found the toast instead!

"At last!" he cried happily. "Now where's the marmalade?"

But his delight turned to dismay when, finding his glasses and putting them on, he discovered that he wasn't on the floor at all—he was on the ceiling with the toast!

"Now what's happening?" he cried, cowering in fright as the toaster suddenly leapt onto the ceiling beside him! (5)

5

Suddenly everything went dark and Penfold got the nasty feeling that he was flying through the air. He could see points of light—like stars. They couldn't be stars! He tried putting his glasses on the other way up. That was better! Now he could see something he recognised. It was the Earth. It was right below him—and getting smaller every second! Penfold fainted.

When he came to, an eerie, unfamiliar landscape met his gaze. Here and there he could see craters of rock and, on one side, a high wall of cliffs with several dark-looking caves.

"W-where am I?" he said nervously, his teeth chattering. He always talked aloud to himself when he was frightened—it made him feel less alone.

"It must be the M-Moon, I suppose," he muttered. "It's not M-Mayfair, that's for sure!"

He was just wondering what to do next, when he heard a shout from the direction of the cliffs. To his amazement, he saw Dangermouse standing in the entrance to one of the caves.

"Oh thank goodness!" he cried happily. He scrambled to his feet, but in his haste tripped over a metal object on the ground.

It was the toaster—and beside it were the two pieces of toast! He looked at them hungrily and, before he could stop himself, gave a loud hiccup!

"Maybe there's time to eat the toast before my hiccups get any worse," (9) he thought. "Or perhaps I should join Dangermouse right away!" (3)

6

"Better stay here and wait for him," thought Penfold. "I'm sure he won't be long." At that moment an army of robots appeared, picked up the ship with Penfold in it, and began to carry it towards the cliffs.

"Put me down!" squealed Penfold. "There's a law against this, you know!"

The robots took no notice and marched swiftly into the nearest cave. Penfold gazed warily around him and was amazed to see Dangermouse striding along behind the ship.

"Thank goodness!" he cried. "I *knew* he'd come to my rescue!"

The robots came to an abrupt halt and Penfold was thrown against the instrument panel, accidentally firing one of the main jets. A burst of flame flared from the engine, and the ship shot forward into the wall.

"Oh crumbs, that's torn it!" he cried. "I'll never get the hang of driving this thing!"

Outside the ship, the robots were lying around on the floor struggling to get up.

"Now's my chance to escape," thought Penfold desperately. "I only hope Dangermouse is all right!"

He looked back and to his horror saw that what he thought was Dangermouse was now nothing but a smoking heap of metal and wires.

"C-crikey!" he quavered. "It was a robot all the time! No wonder he acted so strangely! But what am I going to do now?"

Penfold thought so hard that his glasses steamed up. He thought he had two choices.

Should Penfold try to find a hiding place further inside the cave (13), or should he go back towards the craters where he last saw the real Dangermouse? (12)

7

"Maybe you're right," sighed Penfold. "I'll just take some peppermints to keep me going!"

The space hopper soared into the sky and our intrepid heroes soon sighted the green cloud.

"That's funny!" said Dangermouse, checking his instruments. "We're going at nearly top speed, but we don't seem to be catching that cloud at all! It feels as if it's pulling us along by some sort of magnetic force!"

Penfold wasn't at all happy. Heights always made him dizzy, and the cloud seemed to be taking them higher and higher.

"It's no good, Penfold," said Dangermouse grimly, as he wrestled in vain with the controls. "We're trapped by that cloud and there's nothing I can do about it!"

"We could always panic!" suggested Penfold helplessly.

"Come along, old chap," said Dangermouse. "Remember who we are! Besides, I'm sure to think of something!"

"Well you'd better hurry up, chief," wailed Penfold. "It looks as if we're heading for outer space!"

"We certainly seem to be on course for the Moon at any rate," said Dangermouse. "And I'm beginning to suspect that our old enemy, Greenback, must be behind all this!"

Penfold covered his eyes as the Moon grew larger and larger in front of them.

"Hang on, Penfold," said Dangermouse. "You'd better brace yourself for a bumpy landing!" (8)

8

"Waagh! Help!" cried Penfold desperately, as the space hopper crashed onto the bleak surface of the Moon.

"Calm down, Penfold," ordered Dangermouse. "Not quite as smoothly as I'd have liked, but at least we're down in one piece!"

Penfold peered timidly around him. To one side he could see several large craters, while on the other was a high wall of cliffs and a number of dark-looking caves.

"I don't like the look of this place," he muttered with a shiver. "At least we seem to have escaped that cloud though!"

"I wouldn't be so sure," said Dangermouse darkly. "I'm going outside to have a look round. You'd better stay here and guard the ship."

"All right, chief," said Penfold, much relieved. The thought of what might lie outside the safety of the ship gave him the creeps.

He watched Dangermouse walking away towards the nearest crater. A long time passed, but he didn't return.

"Why does he always leave me on my own?" whimpered Penfold. "He *knows* I can't cope!"

He looked towards the cliffs and was surprised to see Dangermouse standing by one of the caves. He waved, but Dangermouse took no notice.

"That's funny," thought Penfold. "I'm *sure* he went in the opposite direction to look round the craters!"

Should Penfold stay with the ship as he was told to do (6), or should he go and see if Dangermouse is all right? (3)

9

Penfold picked up the toast, but it had gone cold and soggy.

"It was only half done as well!" he grumbled. He looked at the toaster but there was nowhere to plug it in.

"It only needs crisping up a bit," he thought. "Perhaps Dangermouse knows where I can find a power point."

He looked up and to his surprise saw Dangermouse striding towards him.

"Hurry up, Penfold," said Dangermouse urgently. "There's something devilish going on here, and I'm sure Greenback is behind it all."

"But how did we get here?" asked Penfold curiously.

"No time to explain," said Dangermouse briskly. "But it's not safe to stay out here. We must hide in those caves. Come on!"

As he spoke, a small army of robots appeared and began to advance towards them. Dangermouse raced off towards the caves, with Penfold trying hard to keep up with him.

"Can't you run any faster?" cried Dangermouse. "They're gaining on us! And why have you brought that tin box?"

"My toast has gone cold," explained Penfold, still clutching the toaster. "I thought we might find somewhere to plug it in!"

"Toast?" echoed Dangermouse. "What's toast?"

Penfold looked at him uneasily. Something was wrong, but he wasn't quite sure what.

Should Penfold follow Dangermouse (14), or should he be looking for a way to escape? (11) He had a nasty feeling that he was running into a trap!

10

Penfold found himself in a passage with a door at the end marked 'STRICTLY PRIVATE'. He knew that meant you weren't supposed to go in but, summoning up all his courage, he pushed the door open and cautiously peered inside. The first thing he saw was Dangermouse.

"Gosh, chief, am I glad to see *you*!" he cried. "But . . . ?"

He stopped short as first two Dangermice, then three, then four, came into view. Behind them was a row of Colonel K's, and beyond that were rows of people whom Penfold vaguely recognised as being famous.

He froze in his tracks as a horribly familiar voice broke the silence.

"Come in, come in!" hissed the voice malevolently. "Come and join your friend. Or, should I say 'friends'—there are several of each of them!"

"G-Greenback!" quavered Penfold in terror. "So D-Dangermouse was right!"

He took another look at the row of Dangermice. There were six of them!

"They can't *all* be Dangermouse," he muttered in confusion. "Perhaps none of them is. They might all be robots!"

"Don't stand out there in the cold," sneered the toad with an evil laugh. "We're all having *such* fun in here!"

Penfold looked into the room, and then back down the passage. It was empty.

Should Penfold go into the room in the hope that one of the robots is the real Dangermouse (19), or should he try to escape back down the passage? (17)

11

"I wish I could figure it out!" thought Penfold, as he panted along behind Dangermouse. "There's something about him that just isn't quite right!"

"Come on, Penfold," called Dangermouse. "It's not far now!"

"It *sounds* like him all right," pondered Penfold. "It even *looks* like him—right down to his eye patch!"

He stopped dead in his tracks. That was it! He was wearing his eye patch over his right eye! The wrong eye!

"Look, Penfold," snapped Dangermouse impatiently. "Are you coming or not?"

Penfold ran to catch up, but in his haste tripped over a small rock. The toaster flew out of his hands and landed squarely on Dangermouse's foot.

"Oh no!" groaned Penfold. "*Now* he'll be cross with me!"

But instead of a yell of pain, there was a dull clunk. Penfold watched in amazement as Dangermouse's leg crackled and sparked, his foot dangling off by a jumble of wires. It was nothing but a robot!

"C-crumbs!" stammered Penfold. "Er, terribly sorry, but I really must be going!"

He started to run, with the robot limping after him in pursuit. Ahead of him lay a large cave, which seemed to be glowing with a greenish light.

"Well at least it wouldn't be dark," thought Penfold. "The only other place to hide is in those craters over there."

Should Penfold hide in the cave (13), or should he head for one of the craters? (16)

12

Penfold ran towards the nearest crater, leaving the struggling robots behind him. There was still no sign of Dangermouse, but Penfold thought it would be a safe place to hide while he tried to think out his next move.

He scrambled cautiously over the rim of the crater and settled down on a small ledge inside.

"That's better!" he breathed. "At least I can sit here in peace for a while without being seen."

He took off his glasses to clean them properly and immediately wished he hadn't. Putting them back on, he found himself sitting on the edge of a deep black hole, with nothing but a few loose stones between him and a long drop!

What a terrible shock! Before he could help himself, he hiccuped loudly twice and the stones started to slide.

"Waagh! Help!" he cried, scrabbling desperately to keep from slipping, but it was no use. With a wild yell, he slid towards the hole and plunged over the edge. He fell and slid and bounced downwards for what seemed ages before coming to rest with a bump in a small underground cave.

"Well, that's one way of curing hiccups!" he snorted, brushing himself down. By the dim green light of the glowing rock of its walls he could see two passages leading off from the cave in different directions.

"Now which should I choose?" he wondered. "The one that leads upwards (10), or the one that slopes down?" (15)

13

Penfold ran towards the back of the cave which soon split into a maze of tunnels and passages. The rocks seemed to glow with hundreds of green crystals.

"Crikey!" he whined. "It all looks the same to me. I'll never find my way around!"

He went through his pockets to see if there was anything he could use to help him.

"Ah, my trusty penknife!" he cried. "Maybe I can mark out a route on the tunnel walls."

He tried scratching arrows on the walls, but the rock was too hard. After breaking two blades, he gave up.

"That's no good!" he said crossly. "And all I've got left are some peppermints!"

He began to make a trail of the sweets along the floor, but that didn't work either. They were the same colour as the crystals, and soon Penfold couldn't tell which were which. He made his way slowly back trying to find the peppermints, but after nearly breaking his teeth on two of the crystals, he gave up in despair.

"I'll never find my way out of here!" he wailed miserably. "And I'll never find Dangermouse either!"

He took a last good look around him and noticed two passages larger than the rest that led off in different directions.

"Which should I choose?" he asked himself. "The one leading upwards (10), or the one that slopes down?" (15)

14

Shrugging his shoulders, Penfold followed Dangermouse towards the caves. He couldn't think of anywhere else he could escape to, and besides, he couldn't run very fast anyway.

He noticed that the walls inside the nearest cave were glowing with a strange green light. It reminded him that he had a bag of peppermints in his jacket pocket. He *still* hadn't had anything to eat and he was sure that running would bring on his hiccups at any minute.

"Hey, hang on, chief," he panted. "Will you hold this for a second while I find my peppermints?"

He handed Dangermouse the toaster and watched in astonishment as it began to glow red hot in his hands.

"Gosh, chief, you're a genius!" he cried. "That'll crisp up the toast!"

Dangermouse made no reply. Instead, smoke began to pour out of his ears and his head started to spin round alarmingly. With a loud bang, his head finally flew off and his body crashed into the wall with a blue flash.

"Crikey!" exclaimed Penfold, gazing open-mouthed at the smouldering heap of metal and wires. "He was a robot all the time! I *thought* there was something funny about him!"

He peered cautiously into the cave. It was empty. Maybe now he could make his escape.

Should Penfold try to hide in the cave (13), or would he be safer outside, perhaps hiding in one of the craters? (16)

15

Penfold crept slowly down the passage. It seemed to be leading deeper and deeper underground, and Penfold was sure that the green light was somehow getting brighter. From a long way off he seemed to hear the sound of many voices and great activity.

"Well, at least this wretched passage must be leading *somewhere*," he muttered aloud to himself.

"Quite-a right, my friend!" cackled an all too familiar voice. "It-a lead to your doom!"

Penfold spun round and there stood the evil Stiletto, a wicked grin on his face.

"You will-a come with me," said the crow menacingly. "And you not-a try da funny business, OK?"

Stiletto marched Penfold even deeper underground until they came to a series of large caverns.

"You stop-a here!" ordered the crow. "In-a fact," he added with a snigger, "you stop-a here for the rest of-a your life!"

Penfold looked around him. The caverns were full of famous people, hard at work digging the green crystals out of the rock and loading them into trucks. He spotted Colonel K hacking at the walls with a pick, and everywhere he looked there were robot guards on patrol.

"Welcome to the Barone's crystal mines!" sneered Stiletto nastily. "You'd-a better get used to it — there's-a no way of escape!" (18)

16

"I'm sure I'd get lost in all those tunnels," thought Penfold, as he ran towards the craters.

He had completely forgotten the army of robots that he'd seen earlier, and realised suddenly that they were almost on top of him.

He began to panic. Worse than that, his glasses steamed up. To cap it all, he started to hiccup.

"Oh crikey!" he wailed. "I *knew* this would happen if I had to run on an empty stomach!"

He stopped short and fished in his pocket for one of his bright green, triple-strength peppermints.

"This should do the trick!" he thought with a smile. "Dangermouse always says that the colour alone would stop anyone's hiccups!"

He was about to pop it into his mouth, when it was snatched from his hand.

"Hey, what's going on?" He wiped the steam from his glasses and was horrified to see one of the robots standing right next to him. With a clunk it dropped the peppermint into its mouth.

"Just you give that back, you overgrown tin box!" cried Penfold angrily. "I bet *you* haven't got hiccups!"

The robot began to make strange noises and started to spin wildly. It crashed out of control into the other robots, sending them flying.

"Now's my chance," thought Penfold, having regained some of his breath. "I should be able to get to that crater before they see me!" (12)

17

"I'm not going to risk facing Greenback on my own!" thought Penfold nervously. He edged slowly away from the doorway, turned and ran back down the passage.

He looked anxiously over his shoulder and was relieved to see that no one was following him. He turned a corner and immediately realised why.

Right in front of him stood the ruthless Stiletto!

"You will-a come with me," said the crow threateningly. "And you not-a try da funny business, OK?"

Stiletto marched Penfold deeper and deeper underground. Finally the passage opened out into a series of large caverns, all lit with the same green light.

“You stop-a here!” ordered the crow. “In-a fact,” he added with a snigger, “you stop-a here for the rest of your-a life!”

Penfold looked around him. The caverns were full of famous people and there was Colonel K, staggering under the weight of a pile of green crystals.

The prisoners were being forced to dig the crystals out of the rock and load them into trucks. There were robot guards everywhere, to make sure that no one tried to escape.

“I hope-a you like your new home!” sneered Stiletto nastily. “Your brave-a friend Dangermouse will-a never find you down-a here!” (18)

18

"Now you get-a da pick and da shovel, and get-a to work!" ordered the crow. He poked Penfold in the ribs and made him jump. His bag of peppermints flew from his pocket into a truck full of crystals, but he managed to scoop most of them back without Stiletto noticing.

"What's going on here?" asked Penfold. "If I can't ever get out, there's no harm in telling me."

"OK, I tell-a you," said the crow. "The Barone, he has-a kidnapped all these famous people with-a his anti-gravity ray, what-a he make from da crystals. Then-a he send back identical robots what-a only do what-a the Barone tell-a them. That-a way he rule the world!"

“Is there a robot of me?” asked Penfold eagerly.

“You make-a da joke?” scoffed the crow. “The Barone only make-a da robots of-a famous people. You not-a nearly important enough!”

“Then why am I here?” said Penfold sulkily. He didn’t like being told he wasn’t important.

“Simple!” sniggered the crow. “You-a here as-a da bait to catch Dangermouse! Now no more questions—you get-a to work!’

Penfold suddenly had an idea.

“I’m sure crows are partial to peppermints,” he thought to himself.

Should Penfold take a pick and shovel and get to work (23), or should he offer Stiletto a peppermint in the hope of getting some lighter work? (25)

19

Penfold edged timidly into the room and came face to face with the leering Greenback and his woolly pet, Nero. He had the uneasy feeling that someone was creeping up behind. He spun round to find Stiletto grinning at him.

"So!" hissed Greenback evilly. "You have discovered my little secret!"

"Er, n-no, n-not at all," stammered Penfold. "I-I was just passing and . . ."

"Silence, fool!" roared the toad. "Let me explain my fiendish plan. You will no doubt have spotted the green crystals—the caves below here are full of them. I have harnessed their power to make an anti-gravity ray, which I have used to kidnap famous people and bring them here. I then make exact robots of them, programmed to obey only

my orders, and send them back to Earth. The world will be at my mercy!"

"You absolute rotter!" cried Penfold defiantly. "But what happens to the real people—and what do you want *me* for?"

"The real people are imprisoned below us, mining the crystals," gloated Greenback. "And you—you're just bait to trap that interfering rodent, Dangermouse! Once he's in my power, the world is doomed!"

"You'll never get away with it!" cried Penfold desperately. "Dangermouse is much too clever!"

"We'll soon see about that!" leered the toad. "Stiletto, take this pathetic creature away and put him to work in the mines!" (20)

20

Before Stiletto could move, Nero began to squeak urgently in Greenback's ear.

"Well spotted, my little pet!" said Greenback warmly, patting Nero on the head. "You're right—one of those robot Dangermice has the patch over the wrong eye. Put it right, Stiletto."

"Si, Barone," obeyed the crow. "Then I take our little friend downstairs!"

He moved to change the eye patch, but the 'robot' suddenly jumped backwards. It wasn't a robot at all. It was Dangermouse!

"OK, Greenback, the game's up!" he cried. "Get behind me, Penfold!"

"Not so fast!" screamed the toad, flying into a rage. "You won't beat me *that* easily! Robots—attack!"

"But, Barone," cried Stiletto urgently. "You forget-a to tell them *who* to attack!"

It was too late. The robots, obeying only Greenback's orders, began to attack the nearest thing they could find—which was each other! The room was filled with sparks and flashes as the robots crashed wildly about in total confusion.

Penfold crept to safety behind a large packing case to avoid being hurt. When the noise died down, he peered cautiously out. Greenback and his henchmen had disappeared, but there was no sign of Dangermouse either! All that remained were a few robots that were still intact.

Should Penfold go and look for Dangermouse (24), or should he wait for him to come back? (22)

21

Safely back on Earth once more, Dangermouse and Penfold were relaxing after their mission. Their peace was suddenly disturbed as the videoscreen flashed on.

"I dare say that'll be Colonel K wanting to congratulate us," grinned Dangermouse.

"What on Earth is going on, DM?" boomed the Colonel, looking red and flustered.

"I thought you said everything was back to normal!"

"Why, whatever's happened, sir?" asked Dangermouse anxiously.

"I've just had Agent 57 on the 'phone," continued the Colonel. "He says that the Prime Minister has announced in Parliament that she's the Archbishop of Canterbury! Worse than that, the President of the United States is claiming to be *you*, DM!"

"Good grief! That's awful!" cried Dangermouse. He looked accusingly at Penfold, who had gone quite pale.

"I thought you said you'd fixed those last robots!" he said.

"Er, well, I-I was only trying to help!" stammered Penfold nervously. He suddenly felt his hiccups coming on and quickly slipped a peppermint into his mouth. With a cry of panic, he floated up to the ceiling.

"By Jove!" exclaimed the Colonel. "How do we get him down?"

"We don't, sir!" said Dangermouse firmly. "It'll be far better if he stays up there while I go back and finish off this job properly!"

"I hope you can," said the Colonel gravely. "Until every last one of those robots is found and destroyed the world may still be in danger."

Penfold didn't like the sound of that. Had Greenback won after all?

"THE END"?

22

"I hope Dangermouse won't be long," thought Penfold. "These robots give me the shivers!"

He picked his way through the debris and gingerly prodded a Colonel K 'look-alike' that was still in one piece.

"Come on, Colonel, smarten yourself up a bit!" he chuckled, straightening the robot's tie. As he did so, he noticed a small metal plate under the collar, beneath which was a mass of wires.

He quickly checked the other robots and they all seemed to be built the same way.

"Perhaps I ought to change some of these wires around," he pondered. "That should fix them. I'd hate any of them to come to life again while I'm still here on my own!"

He had just finished sabotaging the last one when, to his great relief, Dangermouse returned.

"Good news, Penfold!" cried Dangermouse. "I've managed to free all the famous prisoners, and Colonel K's going to take them back to Earth in Greenback's spaceship!"

"But what about Greenback?" queried Penfold.

"I lost him in the caves, I'm afraid," admitted Dangermouse. "But I don't think he'll give us any more trouble. I also managed to destroy the crystal mines with all his robot guards inside, so that puts an end to *his* little game!"

"Well, I've fixed these robots here," boasted Penfold proudly. "So all we need to do now is get back to our ship and we can go home!" (21)

23 "You will-a go with this-a guard here!" ordered Stiletto. He disappeared cackling nastily as Penfold was led away by a robot guard.

"You don't look strong enough for heavy work," grated the guard mechanically. "Soon it is the prisoners' tea break. You will look after the tea urn!"

To Penfold's astonishment, the guard then began to speak in an urgent whisper.

"Just act naturally, Penfold," hissed the guard. "It's me—Agent 57! Now listen carefully. When you hear the whistle for the tea break, turn on the tap of the tea urn and pretend it won't turn off."

"But that will flood the place with tea!" protested Penfold.

"Exactly!" chuckled 57. "It's the only way to stop these robots. The tea gets in their feet, and shorts their wiring. They'll be quite helpless!"

Penfold followed the plan as he'd been told and, sure enough, one by one the robot guards ground to a halt.

"Brilliant!" cried Penfold in admiration. "I'd never have thought of that!"

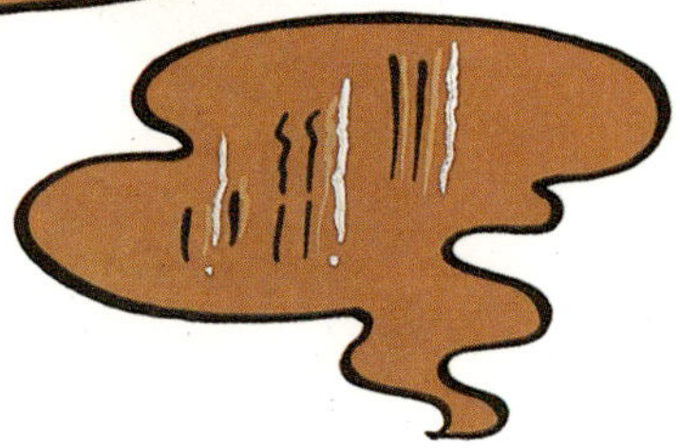

"Oh, it was nothing!" said 57 modestly. "I've managed to steal a plan of the passages. You must make your way to the room marked 'X'—Dangermouse will meet you there!"

Penfold ran off, following the plan as best he could. Suddenly he came to a fork.

"Now should I take the left fork," (28) he wondered, "or could this right one be a short cut?" (31)

24

"Dangermouse can't have gone far," thought Penfold. "He's probably trying to capture the villains. Maybe I should give him a hand."

He ran down the passage a little way and was relieved to see Dangermouse coming towards him.

"Don't worry, Penfold," said Dangermouse with a reassuring grin. "Everything's fine. I've just bumped into Agent 57, who's been up here all the time disguised as a guard. He's freeing all the prisoners right now—they're being taken back to Earth in Greenback's spaceship."

"I say, well done!" cried Penfold proudly. "But what about Greenback?"

"I'm afraid I lost him in the caves," admitted Dangermouse. "But he can't do any more harm. I've destroyed the crystal mines with the robot guards inside, and besides, Greenback will be marooned up here once we've taken his ship!"

"What about those last few robots in there?" asked Penfold, looking back towards Greenback's secret room.

"Oh, I wouldn't worry about those!" chuckled Dangermouse. "I doubt if any of them still work. And anyway, Greenback has no way of getting them back to Earth!"

"Right then," said Penfold happily. "We might as well get back to the ship and return to Earth ourselves. (30) I'm sure Colonel K will be pleased to see us!"

25

"Er, you wouldn't by any chance care for a peppermint?" asked Penfold hopefully, offering the bag to Stiletto.

"So you think I take-a da bribe?" hissed the crow. "Well-a you're wrong—but I take-a da peppermint all the same!"

He snatched a peppermint from the bag and swallowed it greedily. With a startled cry, he floated up to the roof of the cavern.

"Crikey!" exclaimed Penfold in surprise. "I knew they were strong, but this is ridiculous!"

He looked into the bag and noticed that some of the green crystals were mixed up with the peppermints.

“It must have happened when I dropped them into that truck of crystals,” he thought. “I’ll have to be careful I don’t eat any myself!”

“Hey! Get-a me down! I’m-a stuck!” cried Stiletto angrily. “The Barone, he not-a going to like this!”

“Not a chance!” chuckled Penfold. “I’m sure the rest will do you good!”

He looked around him, not quite sure what to do next.

He didn’t notice one of the guards creeping up silently behind him. (26)

26

"Oh crikey, that's torn it!" cried Penfold in despair, as the robot guard laid a hand on his shoulder. "Looks like I'll have to surrender!"

"Don't panic!" whispered the guard urgently. "I'm not really a robot. It's me—Agent 57!"

"But what are *you* doing here?" cried Penfold in amazement.

"No time to explain now," said 57. "And keep your voice down. Pretend to struggle with me, we'll be out of here in no time!"

The plan worked perfectly. Agent 57 captured Penfold, then marched him past the real robot guards to the safety of the passages outside the mines.

"I say, well done!" cried Penfold in admiration. "However did you manage to think of that?"

"Oh, it was nothing," said 57 modestly. "All part of the training, you know!"

"So what's the plan now?" asked Penfold, highly glad to have escaped the mines.

"I've managed to steal a map of these passages," explained 57. "You need to get to the room marked 'X'. Dangermouse will meet you there. But hurry—there's no time to lose!"

Penfold raced off, clutching the map. He'd been going for about five minutes, when he came to a fork. He peered at the map closely.

"It looks as if I can either take the left fork," (32) he muttered, "or take a short cut by turning right." (28)

27

Home once more, Dangermouse and Penfold were making their final report to Colonel K on the videoscreen.

"So Greenback got away, you say?" snorted the Colonel.

"Well, not exactly, sir," chuckled Dangermouse. "As we were leaving the Moon, I noticed him and his henchmen running for all they were worth!"

"Couldn't you have gone after them?" asked the Colonel.

"I didn't think we needed to!" grinned Dangermouse. "There were a hundred robots hot on their heels already!"

"Oh, I see!" cried the Colonel with a hearty laugh. "So the toad's well and truly in a hole, eh? In that case, I reckon you two have earned a holiday!"

"Gosh, thanks, sir!" cried Penfold excitedly. "I haven't been to the seaside for ages!"

"Oh, by the way, Penfold," added the Colonel. "On the way out of those wretched mines, I found your bag of peppermints. Mind if I have one?"

"Go right ahead, sir!" grinned Penfold.

The Colonel popped one into his mouth and with a startled cry floated up to the ceiling.

"Oh crumbs!" cried Penfold. "It must have been one of those crystals!"

"Help! Get me down!" blustered the Colonel furiously. "This is outrageous!"

"It'll wear off in an hour or so!" said Penfold, grinning broadly at Dangermouse. "He's not taking this lightly, is he, chief?"

"The trouble is," chuckled Dangermouse, "he just doesn't seem to understand the gravity of the situation!"

THE END

28

Penfold ran on for a while following the map and finally came to the room marked 'X'.

"Well at least I managed to do *something* right!" he muttered.

He pushed open the door and was astonished to find the room full of famous people — several of each of them! There were even six Dangermice!

"These must be Greenback's 'look-alike' robots!" he decided.

At that moment he heard footsteps outside. To his dismay, it wasn't Dangermouse who entered, but the evil Greenback himself!

"Don't panic, Penfold!" chuckled Dangermouse, appearing from behind the door. "It's only a robot! Agent 57 found it in a store room. Greenback's so vain, it looks as though he made a look-alike of himself!"

"C-crikey!" stammered Penfold. "It certainly had *me* fooled!"

"57's reprogrammed it," explained Dangermouse. "Just watch this!"

He pressed a button and the robot began to speak, just like Greenback.

"Attention, robots!" it hissed. "This is your creator, Baron Greenback speaking."

The other robots were immediately activated by the voice and turned to face Greenback.

"When I leave this room," continued the robot, "you are to wait for five minutes, then follow me. You must then seek and destroy me and disregard any other orders!"

With a final leer, the robot Greenback turned and walked out of the room. (29)

29

"I just don't get it, chief!" said Penfold blankly. "Where's he going now?"

"Agent 57 will lock him back in the store-room," explained Dangermouse slowly. "Which will leave the real Greenback to face all those robots!"

"But where *is* Greenback?" asked Penfold.

"I'm afraid I lost him in the caves," admitted Dangermouse. "But I'm banking on the robots being able to flush him out!"

At that moment, Agent 57 burst into the room.

"Everything's under control, DM," he reported. "I've managed to free all the prisoners from the mines and they're all safely aboard Greenback's ship, waiting for me to take them back to Earth."

"Good work, 57!" beamed Dangermouse. "And what about the crystal mines?"

"I've set all the explosive charges," replied 57. "The whole place should blow at any minute—with all the robot guards inside!"

"Then we've no time to lose!" cried Dangermouse. "Come on, Penfold, we've got to get to the ship—and fast!"

"Good luck, DM!" called 57 as they raced away. "See you back on Earth!"

"I shan't miss this place one bit!" muttered Penfold, as they ran back through the passages to where the rocket car was waiting. "It's put me off peppermints for life!"

With a roar, the car shot into the air, with our two heroes safely aboard and heading for home. (27)

30

"Gosh, it's good to be home!" sighed Penfold contentedly, as he and Dangermouse relaxed after their mission. "The thought of being stuck up there on the Moon makes me feel quite ill!"

"But everything's all right now," said Dangermouse. "I expect the Colonel will want to congratulate us on our success!"

"Why don't we celebrate now?" grinned Penfold. "There's some lemonade in the fridge!"

"Well don't overdo it!" chuckled Dangermouse, as Penfold eagerly poured two large glasses. "You *know* it makes you tipsy!"

Seconds later, the videoscreen flashed on and Colonel K appeared.

"Right, you two!" he blared. "You've interfered with our friend Greenback's plans once too often. You're fired, the pair of you!"

Penfold stood in shocked silence. Had he heard the Colonel correctly or had he had too much lemonade?

"W-what do you make of that, chief?" he asked, shaking his head in disbelief.

Dangermouse said nothing. Instead, bubbles began to come out of his ears and he started to spin round with a strange clanking noise. Penfold noticed with a gasp of horror that his patch was on the wrong eye!

"Oh no!" he cried. "First Colonel K and now Dangermouse! They're both robots!"

He immediately felt his hiccups coming on, and then came the final blow.

"I'm doomed!" he wailed, desperately scrabbling in his pockets. "Not only has Greenback won — but I've run out of peppermints as well!"

THE END

31

"That must be the first right decision I've made since I got here!" grinned Penfold, as he arrived without further trouble at the room marked 'X'.

He walked inside and his mouth dropped open in surprise. The room was full of famous people—but several of each one! There were even six Dangermice!

"Crumbs!" he cried. "These must be Greenback's 'look-alike' robots that Stiletto was telling me about!"

There was no sign of the real Dangermouse, so Penfold took a closer look at the robots. Each one had a small panel on its back.

"I wonder what these are?" he said, prising off the nearest panel to reveal a mass of wires underneath. "I bet if I pull out a few of these, it'll fix these robots for good. Dangermouse *will* be pleased!"

He had just finished sabotaging the robots when Dangermouse arrived.

"These won't cause any more trouble!" said Penfold proudly.

"Pity," said Dangermouse. "I was going to reprogramme them against Greenback, but never mind. You were only trying to help!"

"Where *is* Greenback?" asked Penfold anxiously.

"Still hiding somewhere in these caves," said Dangermouse. "But he can't get far. Agent 57 has taken his spaceship and has gone back to Earth with all the prisoners."

"So all we need to do," said Penfold happily, "is to get back to our own ship and go home!" (21)

32

"I'm bound to get lost if I take the short cut!" muttered Penfold, turning left down the passage.

To his surprise, he ran straight into Dangermouse coming from the opposite direction.

"I thought I was supposed to meet you in the room marked 'X'," said Penfold.

"No time to explain now," said Dangermouse urgently. "We're running out of time. The mines could explode at any second!"

"Crikey!" cried Penfold. "What's been happening?"

"Well, Greenback has given us the slip, I'm afraid," explained Dangermouse. "But I've managed to destroy all his 'look-alike' robots. Agent 57 has freed all the prisoners from the mines and he's going to take them back to Earth in Greenback's spaceship."

"But what about the robot guards?" asked Penfold.

"Agent 57 has dealt with those too," said Dangermouse. "He's re-wired Greenback's control room. The guards are all guarding each other!"

"So what do we do about Greenback?" queried Penfold.

"I'll explain everything later," said Dangermouse. "All we have to do is stop him reaching our ship, and he'll be trapped up here with no means of escaping!"

"Crumbs! Then we'd better hurry!" cried Penfold. "The sooner we get back to the ship, the quicker we can go home!" (30)